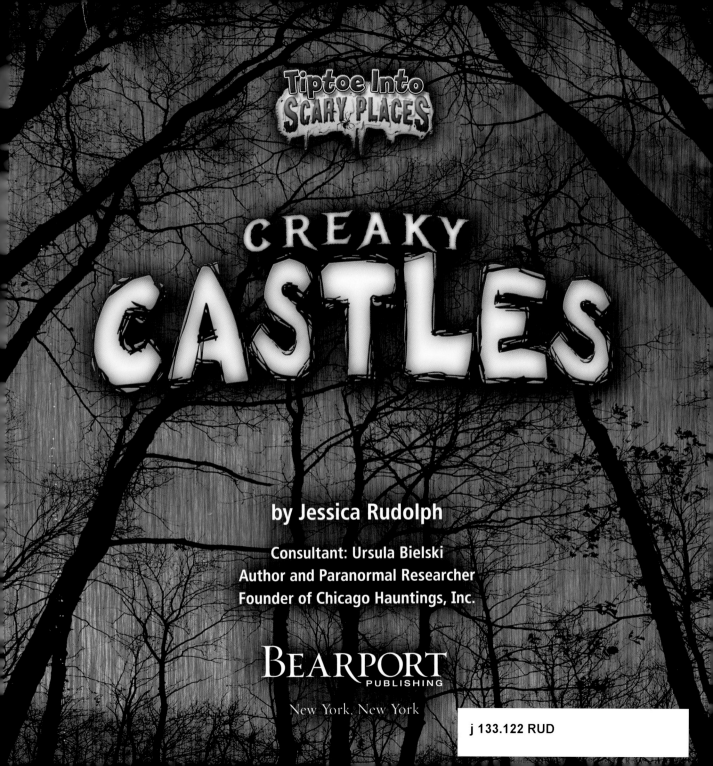

Tiptoe Into SCARY PLACES

CREAKY CASTLES

by Jessica Rudolph

Consultant: Ursula Bielski
Author and Paranormal Researcher
Founder of Chicago Hauntings, Inc.

BEARPORT PUBLISHING

New York, New York

Credits

Cover, © Slavko Sereda/Shutterstock, © Grezova Olga/Shutterstock, and © Fatbob/Bigstockphoto; TOC, © zimmytws/Shutterstock; 4–5, © Carlos Caetano/Shutterstock; 6, © Lumppini/Shutterstock; 7, © Hideo Kurihara/Alamy; 8T, © Elnur/Shutterstock; 8 (L to R), © Bernard Allum/iStock, © Ralf Hettler/iStock, and © Bernard Allum/iStock; 9, © Lidiya/Dreamstime; 10, © Jule_Berlin/Shutterstock; 11, © Kiselev Andrey Valerevich/Shutterstock; 12L, © Fablok/Shutterstock; 12R, © Just2shutter/Shutterstock; 13, © Istvan Csak/Shutterstock and © faestock/Shutterstock; 14, Public Domain; 15, © Justin Black/Shutterstock; 16, © Duncan Walker/iStock; 17, © Artokoloro Quint Lox Limited/Alamy; 18, © Stocktrek Images, Inc./Alamy; 19, © Catalin Petolea/Shutterstock; 20, © Fotokon/Shutterstock; 21, © World History Archive/Alamy; 23, © Pecold/Shutterstock; 24, © Aksenova Natalya/Shutterstock.

Publisher: Kenn Goin
Editor: J. Clark
Creative Director: Spencer Brinker
Photo Researcher: Thomas Persano
Cover: Kim Jones

Library of Congress Cataloging-in-Publication Data

Names: Rudolph, Jessica, author.
Title: Creaky castles / by Jessica Rudolph.
Description: New York, New York : Bearport Publishing Company, Inc., [2017] |
   Series: Tiptoe into scary places | Audience: Age 5–8. | Includes
bibliographical references and index.
Identifiers: LCCN 2016042366 (print) | LCCN 2016045163 (ebook) | ISBN
   9781684020478 (library) | ISBN 9781684020997 (ebook)
Subjects: LCSH: Haunted castles—Juvenile literature.
Classification: LCC BF1474 .R83 2017 (print) | LCC BF1474 (ebook) | DDC
   133.1/22—dc23
LC record available at https://lccn.loc.gov/2016042366

For more information, write to Bearport Publishing Company, Inc., 45 West 21st Street, Suite 3B, New York, New York 10010. Printed in the United States of America.

10 9 8 7 6 5 4 3 2 1

CONTENTS

CREAKY CASTLES

A full moon rises above a castle's crumbling walls. Bats swoop out of a tall stone tower. You wonder—what terrors wait for you inside the dark **fortress**? Could ghosts be wandering the hallways? Maybe there's even a bloodthirsty creature locked up in the dungeon!

4

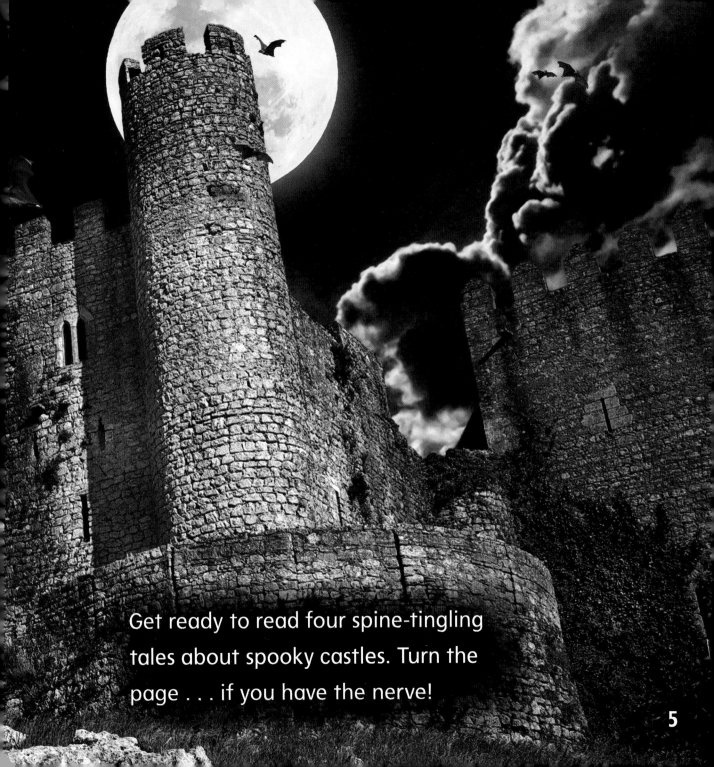

Get ready to read four spine-tingling tales about spooky castles. Turn the page . . . if you have the nerve!

A Waterfall of Blood

Hachioji Castle, Tokyo, Japan

Castles often have large armies to protect them. Yet what happens when the armies leave? Then the people inside are helpless.

In 1590, an army of fierce **samurai** attacked Hachioji Castle.

Most of Hachioji's soldiers were away fighting another battle. The women in the castle knew they would be captured and **tortured**. What could they do?

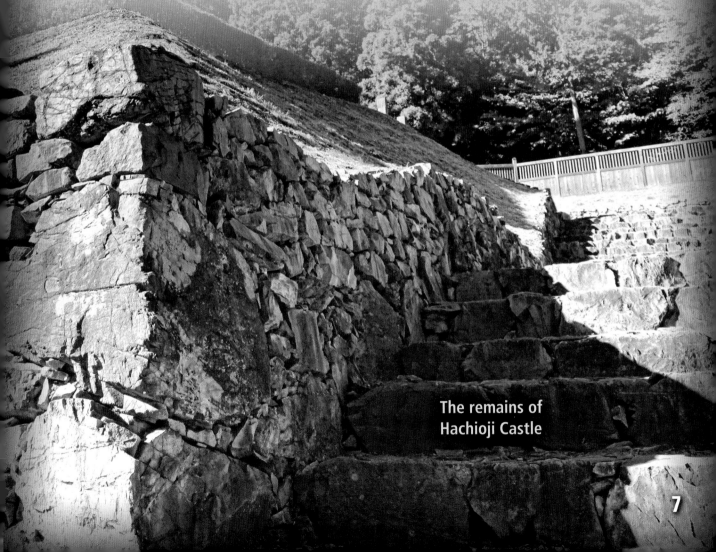

The remains of Hachioji Castle

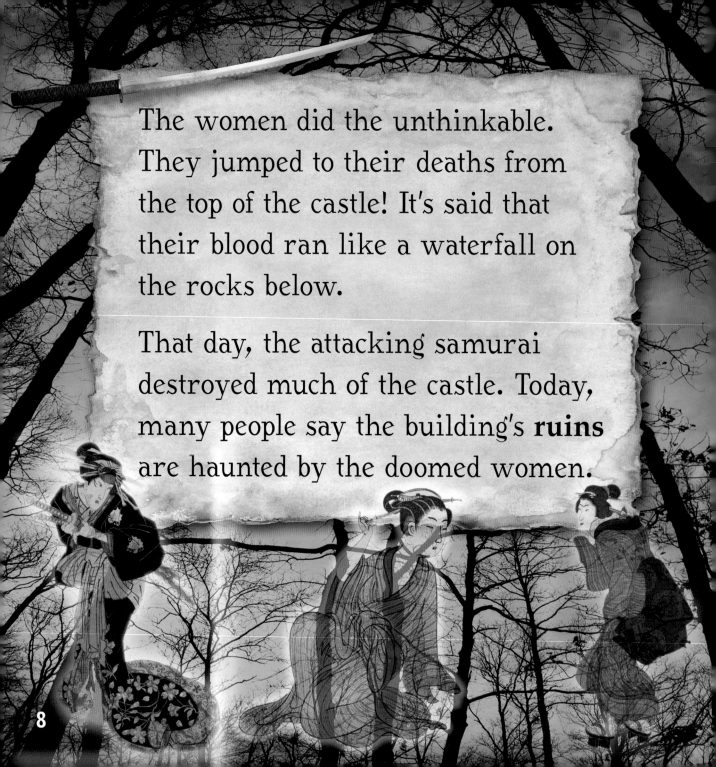

The women did the unthinkable. They jumped to their deaths from the top of the castle! It's said that their blood ran like a waterfall on the rocks below.

That day, the attacking samurai destroyed much of the castle. Today, many people say the building's **ruins** are haunted by the doomed women.

Visitors report hearing the ghostly screams of women and the deadly thud of bodies hitting the rocks.

9

A Hidden Vampire

Glamis Castle, Angus, Scotland

Vampires are undead **supernatural** beings. They attack the living and drink their blood. Glamis Castle may have a vampire lurking inside.

Glamis Castle

In the 1400s, the castle's owners caught a servant girl sucking a victim's blood. The girl was a vampire! The frightened owners locked the creature in a secret room. With no food or water, they hoped she would die.

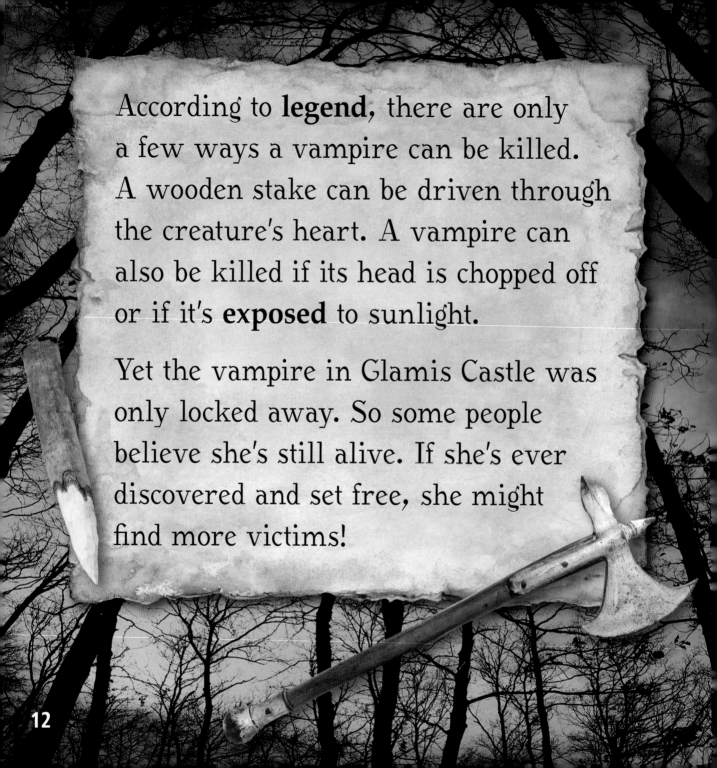

According to **legend**, there are only a few ways a vampire can be killed. A wooden stake can be driven through the creature's heart. A vampire can also be killed if its head is chopped off or if it's **exposed** to sunlight.

Yet the vampire in Glamis Castle was only locked away. So some people believe she's still alive. If she's ever discovered and set free, she might find more victims!

Glamis Castle is also haunted by ghosts. One spirit was accused of being a witch when she was alive. She was burned at the stake in the 1500s.

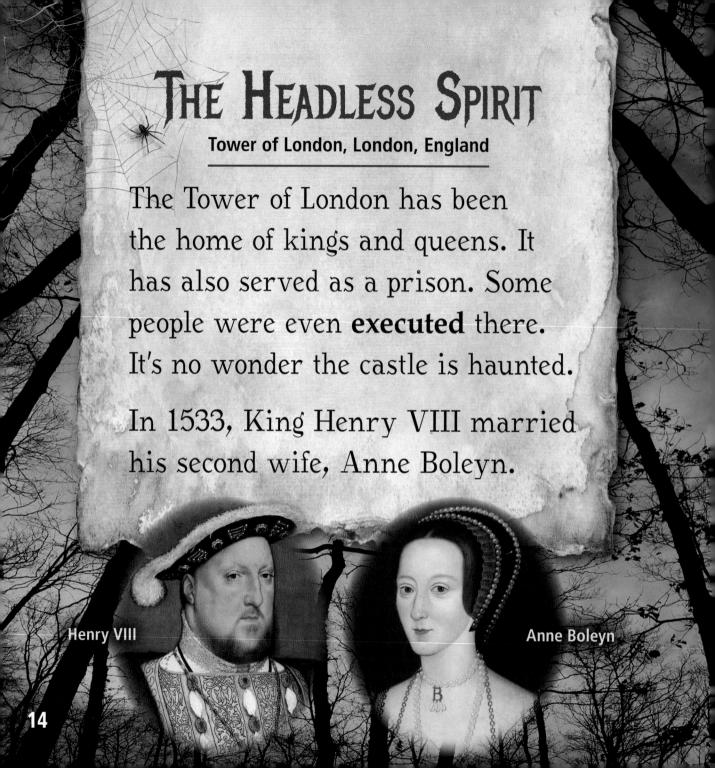

THE HEADLESS SPIRIT

Tower of London, London, England

The Tower of London has been the home of kings and queens. It has also served as a prison. Some people were even **executed** there. It's no wonder the castle is haunted.

In 1533, King Henry VIII married his second wife, Anne Boleyn.

Henry VIII

Anne Boleyn

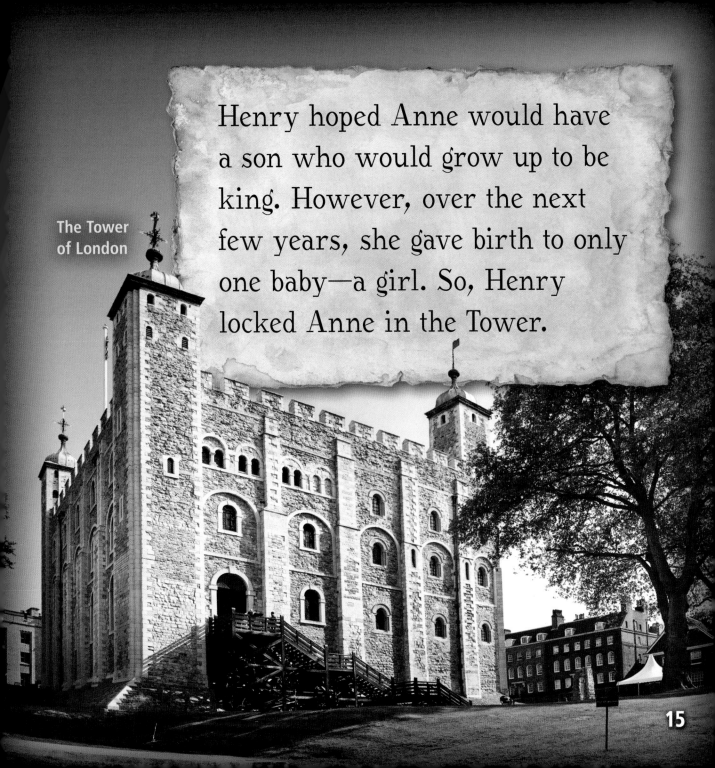

Henry hoped Anne would have a son who would grow up to be king. However, over the next few years, she gave birth to only one baby—a girl. So, Henry locked Anne in the Tower.

The Tower of London

On May 19, 1536, Anne was taken from her prison room to the Tower's lawn, where a crowd had gathered. Anne was ordered to kneel down. Then a swordsman sliced her head off in one blow.

Today, some visitors to the Tower say Anne's headless spirit roams the castle. She's even been seen carrying her own head!

Vlad the Impaler

Poienari Castle, Arges County, Romania

In 1447, Prince Vlad's father and brother were murdered. The **noblemen** who were supposed to defend his family had done nothing. Vlad was furious. He spent years thinking up a terrible revenge.

One day in 1457, Vlad rounded up the families of the noblemen. He brought them to his crumbling castle high in the mountains.

Prince Vlad

Then Vlad forced them to carry huge rocks to rebuild the castle walls. Some were worked to death.

Poienari Castle

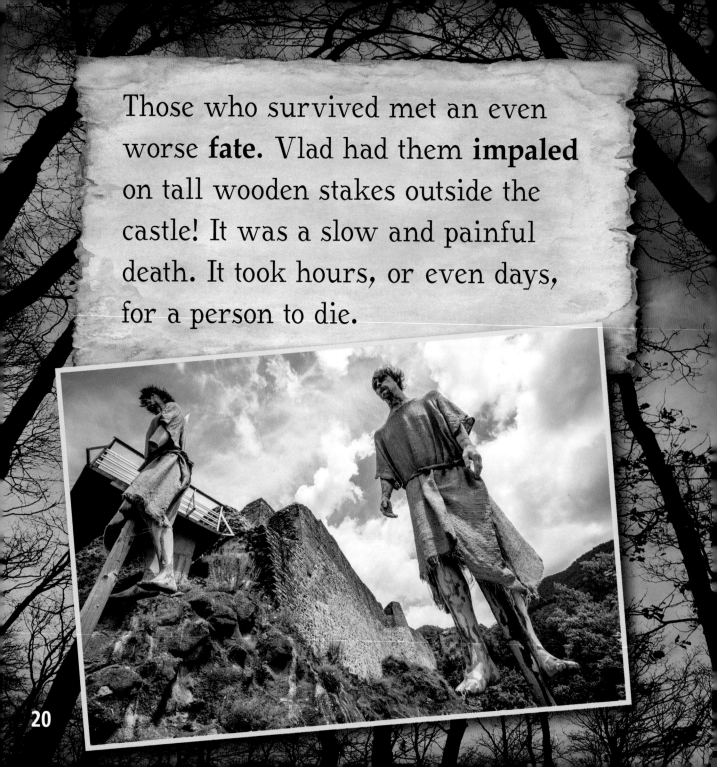

Those who survived met an even worse **fate.** Vlad had them **impaled** on tall wooden stakes outside the castle! It was a slow and painful death. It took hours, or even days, for a person to die.

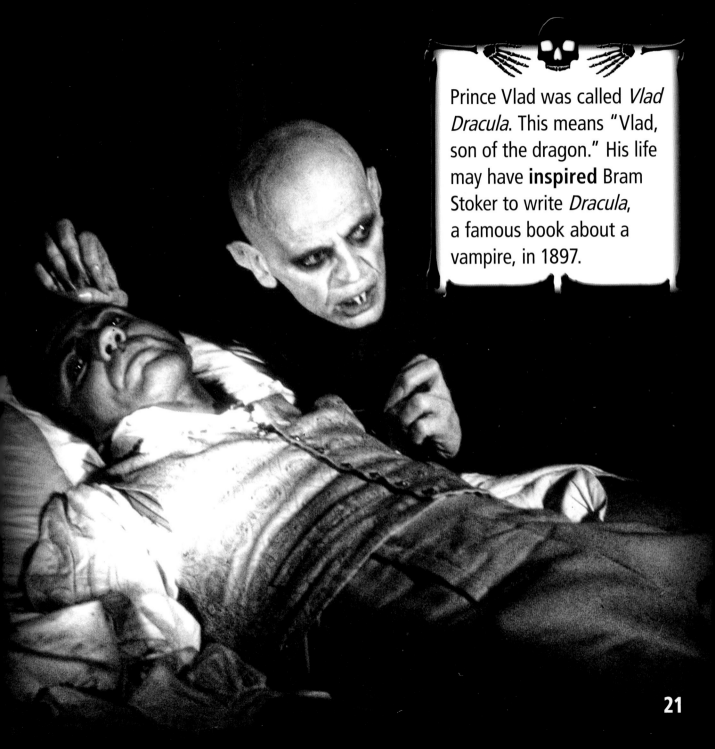

Prince Vlad was called *Vlad Dracula*. This means "Vlad, son of the dragon." His life may have **inspired** Bram Stoker to write *Dracula*, a famous book about a vampire, in 1897.

21

CREAKY CASTLES
AROUND THE WORLD

TOWER OF LONDON
London, England

Walk the halls of a castle that's haunted by a headless spirit.

GLAMIS CASTLE
Angus, Scotland

Could a vampire be locked away in a secret room at this castle?

POIENARI CASTLE
Arges County, Romania

Visit the castle where Prince Vlad impaled his victims.

HACHIOJI CASTLE
Tokyo, Japan

Check out a place where women chose to jump to their deaths rather than be captured.

Arctic Ocean

NORTH AMERICA

EUROPE

ASIA

Atlantic Ocean

Pacific Ocean

AFRICA

Pacific Ocean

SOUTH AMERICA

Indian Ocean

Atlantic Ocean

AUSTRALIA

N
W E
S

Southern Ocean

ANTARCTICA

GLOSSARY

executed (EK-suh-*kyoo*-tid) put to death

exposed (ek-SPOHZD) left without protection from something harmful

fate (FAYT) final result

fortress (FORE-triss) a large building that is made extra strong to withstand attacks

impaled (im-PAYLD) killed by being stabbed with a sharp wooden pole

inspired (in-SPYE-urd) caused someone to do something creative

legend (LEJ-uhnd) a story from the past that is often not entirely true

noblemen (NOH-buhl-men) people of high rank

ruins (ROO-inz) what is left of something that has decayed or been destroyed

samurai (SAM-oo-*rye*) Japanese warriors, or soldiers, who lived in medieval times (the years from the 400s through the 1400s)

supernatural (*soo*-pur-NACH-ur-uhl) something unusual that breaks the laws of nature

tortured (TORE-churd) punished by causing great suffering

INDEX

READ MORE

Owen, Ruth. *Vampires and Other Bloodsuckers (Not Near Normal: The Paranormal).* New York: Bearport (2013).

Phillips, Dee. *The Vampire's Lair (Cold Whispers II).* New York: Bearport (2017).

LEARN MORE ONLINE

To learn more about creaky castles, visit:
www.bearportpublishing.com/Tiptoe

ABOUT THE AUTHOR

Jessica Rudolph is a writer from Connecticut. She has visited spooky castles in Ireland, Scotland, and Germany, but she hasn't seen any ghosts or vampires—yet.